W9-API-429

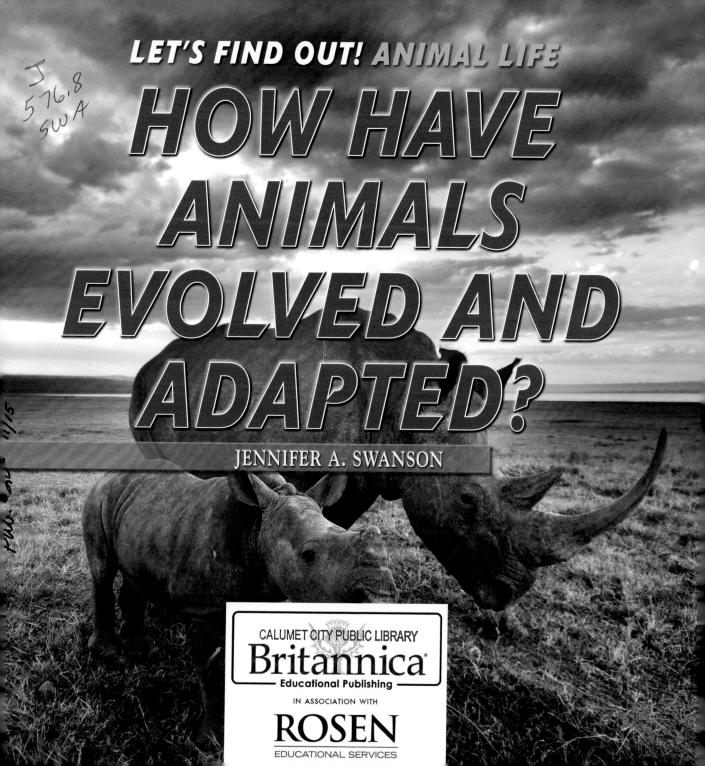

LET'S FIND OUT! ANIMAL LIFE

HOW HAVE ANIMALS EVOLVED AND ADAPTED?

JENNIFER A. SWANSON

Published in 2016 by Britannica Educational Publishing (a trademark of Encyclopædia Britannica, Inc.) in association with The Rosen Publishing Group, Inc.
29 East 21st Street, New York, NY 10010

Distributed exclusively by Rosen Publishing.
To see additional Britannica Educational Publishing titles, go to rosenpublishing.com.

First Edition

Britannica Educational Publishing
J. E. Luebering: Director, Core Reference Group
Mary Rose McCudden: Editor, Britannica Student Encyclopedia

Rosen Publishing
Kathy Kuhtz Campbell: Editor
Nelson Sá: Art Director
Brian Garvey: Designer
Cindy Reiman: Photography Manager

Library of Congress Cataloging-in-Publication Data
Swanson, Jennifer A.
How have animals evolved and adapted?/Jennifer A. Swanson.
        pages cm—(Let's find out! Animal life)
Includes bibliographical references and index.
ISBN 978-1-62275-996-5 (library bound) — ISBN 978-1-62275-997-2 (pbk.) —
ISBN 978-1-62275-999-6 (6-pack)
1. Evolution (Biology)—Juvenile literature. 2. Animals—Adaptation—Juvenile literature. I. Title.
QH367.1.S83 2015
576.8'2—dc23

2014037557

Manufactured in the United States of America

CONTENTS

What Are Evolution and Adaptation?

Have you ever noticed how many different plants and animals live on Earth? They come in all shapes, sizes, and colors. They live in all kinds of places. How did so many different living things come to be?

Scientists believe that plants and animals and other forms of life went through a process called evolution. Evolution is the idea that all living things that exist today developed from earlier types.

The Arctic fox may have evolved from ancient foxes that lived in the mountains of Tibet.

hippopotamus

walrus   duck

Animals such as walrus, hippopotamuses, and ducks developed traits to adapt to their environments.

Evolution takes place over thousands or millions of years. Evolution happens because habitats, or the places where living things usually dwell, change over long periods of time. The environment, or surroundings, may become warmer or colder, or it may change from a swampy area to a desert.

Living things must adapt to survive as their surroundings change. They adapt by developing new **traits**. For example, an animal may have better eyesight or move faster than another animal of its kind. These traits may help it to find food more efficiently and to avoid its enemies. Such useful traits give the animal an advantage over others of its kind.

From Single Cells to Vertebrates

Most scientists believe that the first life forms on Earth were single-celled organisms. They lived more than 3.5 billion years ago in warm, salty pools of water. Over time, these organisms developed into more complex forms.

Over many millions of years, some animals developed bones. At some point, some grew hollow, jointed backbones. They became known as vertebrates, or animals with backbones. (Animals that do not have backbones are called invertebrates.)

Earth's environment continued to change over time. The vertebrates had to adapt to thrive. The animals that lived in the salty ocean water moved to freshwater. Then, as the streams dried up or became shallow, they had

Ancient whales had characteristics similar to land-dwelling animals.

to learn to crawl on land and to breathe air. They developed lung-like structures and fins that could help them crawl. In time, some grew legs and began to walk on land.

Vertebrates that live both in water and on land are called amphibians. Early amphibians were the ancestors of all reptiles, birds, and mammals. Some living amphibians include frogs, toads, salamanders, and wormlike creatures called caecilians. The first animals to live completely on land were reptiles. Dinosaurs are well-known reptiles that died out millions of years ago. Today there are thousands of species, or types, of living reptiles. They include snakes, lizards, turtles and tortoises, alligators, and crocodiles.

Reptiles all have scales on their bodies.

FOSSIL CLUES

The proof of evolution is seen in fossils, the remains of living things. An animal fossil can be an imprint of a bone or other body part (such as a feather) in a stone or in the soil. It can also be the body part itself. Fossils show that many species that once existed were quite different from any kinds that live today. Scientists use animal fossils to determine how today's animals evolved from ancient ones.

They compare the fossil to today's living animal to help them understand how animals lived long ago. Any differences are thought to have happened because of adaptation and evolution.

Dinosaurs are an example of how scientists study fossils.

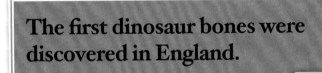

The first dinosaur bones were discovered in England.

Imprint fossils, like this one, show the entire skeleton of an animal.

These lizard-like reptiles lived more than 66 million years ago, but none are alive today.

So how do scientists know that dinosaurs existed? They began to discover dinosaur fossils in the early 1800s. By studying these fossils, scientists now know that dinosaurs were the ancient cousins of today's crocodiles, snakes, and lizards.

When scientists compare some dinosaurs to other reptiles, they see similar traits. These include sharp teeth, long tails, and the way they walked on two or four legs.

THINK ABOUT IT
In what ways do you think dinosaurs could have adapted to stay alive until today?

Darwin and Natural Selection

Charles Darwin was an English scientist who studied nature. He formed the theory of evolution by natural selection. According to this theory, all living things are in a constant struggle to stay alive. The living things that have the most useful traits for existing within their environment tend to survive more often than those with less useful traits.

Polar bears are struggling to survive in a warming climate.

Gerbils live in open, sandy areas, so matching their background is essential for their safety.

When living things with the most useful traits have offspring, the new animals have those helpful traits as well. The process continues with each generation. The animals with the helpful traits survive and continue to increase in number. Those with less useful traits do not adapt well and have fewer offspring. They eventually die out. Darwin called this process natural selection. In this way, animals adapt and evolve over many years.

The process of natural selection can be illustrated with the following example. A sand-colored gerbil living in a sandy desert blends in with its surroundings. Snakes or other enemies will be more likely to see and eat gerbils of other colors. Over time, the gerbils of other colors will die out, leaving only the sandy-colored ones.

MENDEL AND GENETICS

Charles Darwin knew that traits were passed from one generation to another, but he did not know how that happened. In the 1850s and 1860s, an Austrian monk named Gregor Mendel decided to find out. He studied pea plants in his garden. He combined plants with different traits to see which traits would be passed along. Mendel worked out some of the rules that control how a plant grows. He found that there are basic units of heredity that are passed from a parent to its offspring. These are now called genes. Later scientists found that these laws of inheritance were the same for every living thing.

Pod D had to have been the result of a combination of pods A and B or B and C because it has both green and yellow peas.

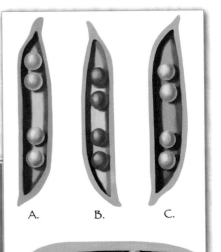

A.   B.   C.

D.

Think About It

Each parent carries two genes for every trait. They give each child only one gene from every pair. Given this, why might offspring of the same parents display different traits?

Genes carry all the information about a living thing, including its traits. Genes exist inside the cells that make up living things. Threadlike structures called chromosomes carry the genes. Most living things have pairs of chromosomes (one comes from each parent). The mother's and father's genes work together to produce the offspring's traits, such as eye and hair color. Each gene has a special job to do, providing the instructions on what the offspring will look like, how it will act in its environment, and so on.

If a child has cheek dimples, she must have inherited a dominant cheek-dimple gene from one of her parents.

Protect and Defend

Animals have several ways of adapting to the sometimes hostile world around them. Some have developed traits to protect themselves. The poison dart frog, for example, produces poison through its skin. Predators trying to eat this amphibian are met with an unpleasant, and deadly, surprise. The bright colors of the poison dart frog warn other animals that it is dangerous and should not be eaten.

VOCABULARY
Predators are animals that live by killing and eating other animals.

Poison dart frogs can be red, orange, yellow, and even bright blue or green.

Most salamanders have poison glands in the skin. The glands are marked by brightly colored areas on the body. The substance released by the glands leaves an unpleasant taste or causes pain in the mouth of a predator. Salamanders can also lash their tails to defend themselves. The tails of some salamanders can break off during an attack. While the wriggling tail distracts an enemy, the victim is free to escape. A new tail will grow to replace the one that was lost.

Mimicry is another trait that animals have developed to defend themselves. Mimicry is when one living thing looks or acts like another living thing. The monarch butterfly tastes bad to predators. Birds learn to avoid it. The viceroy butterfly does not taste bad. However, it has the same orange and black colors of the monarch butterfly's wings. Many birds, therefore, think the viceroy is a monarch butterfly, and they will fly right by.

Adapting for Survival

Animals must eat to survive. When a food source goes away, animals must adapt to a new type of food or die.

Charles Darwin studied a group of finches with medium-sized beaks that lived on an island. They preferred to eat soft-shelled seeds. They pushed aside the hard-shelled seeds because their beaks could not crack them. Other scientists observed that a drought on the island caused a drop in the number of soft-shelled seeds. How could the finches survive?

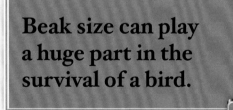

Beak size can play a huge part in the survival of a bird.

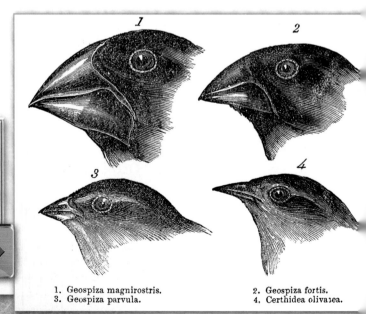

1. Geospiza magnirostris.
2. Geospiza fortis.
3. Geospiza parvula.
4. Certhidea olivasea.

Several finches had been born with slightly larger than normal beaks. They were able to eat the hard-shell seeds with ease. As the drought continued, the finches with the smaller beaks began to die off. The larger-beaked finches survived. As the larger-beaked finches produced offspring, they passed on the helpful larger beak trait to their offspring. The offspring, in turn, passed along the same trait to their young. These finches provide an example of evolutionary change through natural selection.

A finch with a large beak crunches on a seed.

Scientists study a large coelacanth.

A few animals have managed to stay somewhat the same over a long time. The coelacanth is a type of fish that was thought to have died out more than 80 million years ago. In 1938, however, a fisherman caught a coelacanth in his net. Many others have been seen since then. How can this fish still exist? It has adapted to life deep under the ocean, where the conditions do not change much.

Scientists call horseshoe crabs living fossils because their ancient relatives lived more than 400 million years ago. Today's horseshoe crabs have not changed much from the forms that lived about 150 million years ago.

THINK ABOUT IT

How would a coelacanth have to change if its environment changed? How would it be different from the fish that live today?

They were able to find a safe place to live with very few environmental changes. They needed very little adaptation over time. Horseshoe crabs are not crabs at all but are related to scorpions and spiders. They live in shallow sandy or muddy ocean waters. They can be found along the east coasts of Asia and North America.

The horseshoe crab is named for the shape of its head, which looks like a horse's hoof.

Becoming Extinct

When animals cannot adapt, they are in danger of becoming extinct. Plants, animals, and other forms of life sometimes become extinct because of a sudden, serious change in their habitat. Scientists think this may be what happened to the dinosaurs. A meteor hit Earth and sent up a giant cloud of dust that blocked the sunlight from reaching Earth. The plants died because they could not grow without sunlight. The dinosaurs that ate plants died a short time after the plants died.

> **Vocabulary**
> A plant or animal that is **extinct** has died out completely.

The dodo bird became extinct in the 1680s because people hunted it for food.

Extinction can also happen when new predators, such as humans and their domesticated animals, are introduced to the environment. Humans killed many dodos, flightless birds that lived on the island of Mauritius, starting about 1507. By 1681 the last dodo died, and the species became extinct.

Individual animals can become extinct, or there can be mass extinctions. A mass extinction is when many different species, or types, become extinct in a very short time. The worst mass extinction happened about 252 million years ago. This extinction included mainly animals without backbones that lived in water.

Many scientists believe that planet Earth is currently experiencing another mass extinction. This time it is being caused by humans and their activities.

Some people, however, are trying to help protect some of the plants and animals that are in danger of becoming extinct. They may try to protect the habitats of the animals. Or they may help animals breed, or have offspring.

A mother bald eagle feeds her baby in its nest.

Bald eagles were once on the edge of extinction. But through careful watching and breeding programs, they have been saved and have recovered.

Modern-day elephants are related to two animals that became extinct long ago. Mastodons first appeared more than 20 million years ago. They were shorter and heavier than elephants and were covered with long, reddish brown hair.

Woolly mammoths developed later. They lived more than 10,000 years ago. Woolly mammoths were about the same size as elephants, but

Ancient relatives of modern elephants include mastodons and woolly mammoths.

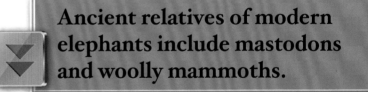

American mastodon   woolly mammoth   African savanna el

◄◄ Scientists study the fossilized remains of a baby woolly mammoth.

they had a long, hairy yellowish coat. Both animals lived in very cold climates and needed their hairy coats to keep warm.

Scientists have been able to study mastodons and woolly mammoths because specimens have been found trapped in ice. They are not sure why these animals became extinct. However, the weather got colder, and ice fields covered the grasslands where the animals fed. Hunting by ancient humans may have played a role in their extinction as well.

COMPARE AND CONTRAST

How are elephants of today similar to their ancient relatives, the mastodons and woolly mammoths? Compare and contrast their tusks, outward appearance, and size. How are they different?

Human Evolution

Scientists have long been interested in how humans evolved on Earth. There are many theories about the beginnings of modern humans. Most scientists believe that humans developed in stages from earlier apelike ancestors that are now extinct.

The bodies of these human ancestors changed over time. In general, their brains became larger. The jaws and teeth became smaller. Human ancestors eventually began walking upright on two feet and using tools. As they did,

The earliest forms of humans evolved from apelike animals.

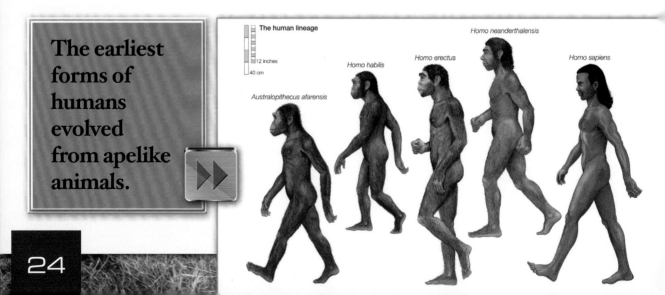

The human lineage

12 inches
40 cm

Australopithecus afarensis

Homo habilis

Homo erectus

Homo neanderthalensis

Homo sapiens

the shape of their legs, feet, hands, and other body parts changed.

Scientists have based these ideas on evidence. This evidence is usually found in the form of fossils. They have found many fossils dating back thousands of years.

Humans did not evolve from apes as we know them today. Instead, modern humans and apes both developed from a common ancestor. The ancestors of humans became separate from the ancestors of apes between eight million and five million years ago. After that, each group developed on its own.

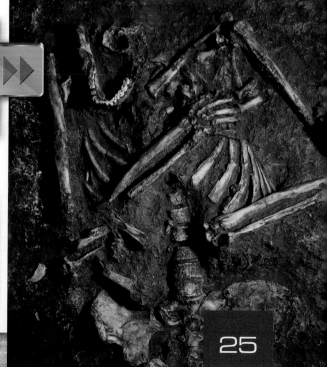

Fossils are used to piece together evidence of how humans evolved.

VOCABULARY
Evidence is something that shows that something else exists or is true.

Homo Sapiens

The ancestors of human beings began to take on the traits of modern humans about two million years ago. These later humans are part of a group that has the scientific name *Homo*, which means "man." Ancient humans behaved much like today's humans. They hunted for food, used tools to build things, and cooked their food.

The species of humans called Neanderthals were alive for part of the same time as modern humans. But they died out about 28,000 years ago. They were closely related to modern humans, but they were not their direct ancestors.

Today's humans probably developed between 200,000 and

Shown here are the heads of axes once used by ancient humans.

COMPARE AND CONTRAST

Ancient humans and modern-day humans had similar and different traits. Compare and contrast their physical features, way of living, and use of tools.

100,000 years ago. The scientific name of modern humans is *Homo sapiens*, which means "wise man."

Many scientists believe that the first modern humans evolved in Africa and then spread through Asia and Europe and later the Americas. The discovery of cave paintings and ancient tools support this theory. But exactly how modern humans emerged is a question that scientists are still studying.

Cave paintings show ancient humans hunting large animals for food.

Never-Ending Cycle

Over many millions of years, some single-celled organisms evolved to become vertebrates. Eventually many different groups of vertebrates developed. Evolution is responsible for all of these developments. It is the process of constant change that helps living things adapt to the environments they dwell in. The differences between the ancient species and today's animals arose gradually. Some took hundreds or even thousands of years to develop.

Crocodiles are the last living link to the dinosaur-like reptiles of prehistoric times.

Over the years, animals have evolved as their environments changed. They learned to adapt to new climates, new threats, and new habitats. They continue to do so today. Through the process of natural selection, traits that help animals survive are passed along to each new generation.

Earth is an ever-changing environment. New animals and plants come to life. Others die out completely. The cycle is never ending.

Ancestors of the modern-day camel lived more than 40 million years ago.

29

GLOSSARY

adaptation A change in a plant or animal that makes it better able to live in a particular place or situation.

ancestors Those from whom an individual, group, or species is descended.

chromosomes The parts of a cell that contain the genes that control how a living thing grows and what it becomes.

climate The usual weather conditions in a particular place or region.

environment The conditions that surround someone or something.

evolution The theory that the differences between modern living things and earlier types are because of changes that happened by a natural process over a very long time.

fossils Remains, such as a leaf, skeleton, or footprint, from plants or animals that lived in ancient times.

genes The parts of a cell that control or influence the appearance, growth, and other features of a living thing.

habitats The places where plants or animals naturally or usually live or grow.

Homo sapiens The human race.

hostile Unfriendly or dangerous.

inheritance The act of offspring receiving genetic traits from parents.

mammal An animal that breathes air, has a backbone, is nourished with milk from special glands of the mother, and grows hair at some point during its life.

natural selection The process by which living things that can adapt to changes in their environment are able to survive and have offspring while those that cannot adapt do not survive.

offspring The young of an animal or plant.

process A series of changes that lead toward a particular result.

species A group of living things having similar traits and a common name.

tortoise A type of turtle that lives on land.

For More Information

Books

Fox, Karen C., and Nancy Davis. *Older Than the Stars*. Watertown, MA: Charlesbridge, 2010.

Gee, Henry, and Luis V. Rey. *A Field Guide to Dinosaurs*. New York, NY: Chartwell Books, 2012.

Parker, Steve. *Adaptation*. 2nd ed. Oxford, UK: Heinemann Library, 2008.

Pringle, Laurence, Steve Jenkins, Jerry A. Coyne, and Carla Weise. *Billions of Years, Amazing Changes: The Story of Evolution*. Honesdale, PA: Boyds Mills, 2011.

Rubino, Michael. *Bang! How We Came to Be*. Amherst, NY: Prometheus Books, 2011.

Websites

Because of the changing nature of Internet links, Rosen Publishing has developed an online list of websites related to the subject of this book. This site is updated regularly. Please use this link to access this list:

http://www.rosenlinks.com/LFO/Evol

INDEX